AF338137

SINGLE-DIGIT SUBTRACTION FOR GRADE 1

MATH WORKBOOKS

Children's Math Books

Let's learn Subtraction!
One of the four basic mathematical operations we use in our daily lives.

Are you ready?

WHAT IS SUBTRACTION?

It is a process of taking something away from a number or group of things. Subtracting one number from another number is used to find the difference between them.

Example:

There are 6 carrots (minuend) to be subtracted by 2 carrots (subtrahend) and the result of that is 4 which is called the difference.

How do you find the difference between 6 carrots and 2 carrots? See below:

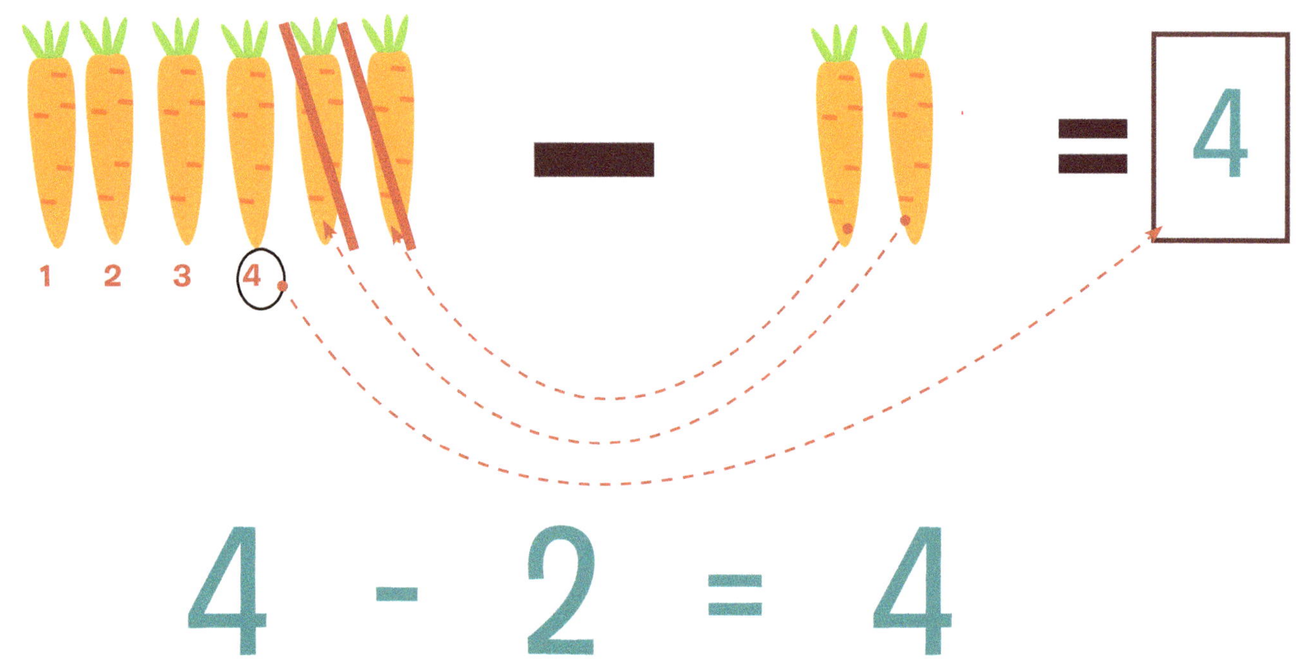

$$4 - 2 = 4$$

It's your turn to subtract!
You can have fun and practice
with these exercises.

Enjoy!

VISUAL SUBTRACTION EXERCISES

Activity No. 1

Find the Difference.

Activity No. 2

Find the Difference.

Activity No. 3

Find the Difference.

Activity No. 4

Find the Difference.

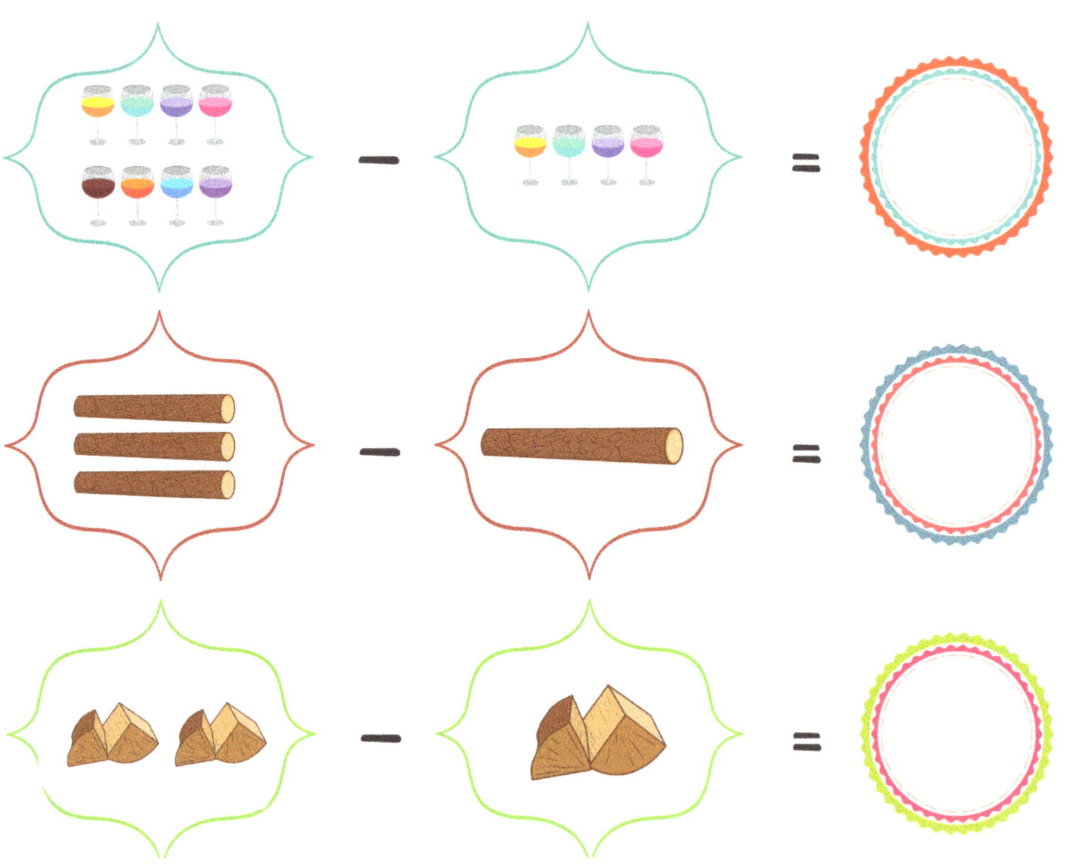

Activity No. 5

Find the Difference.

Activity No. 6

Find the Difference.

Activity No. 7

**Find the Difference.

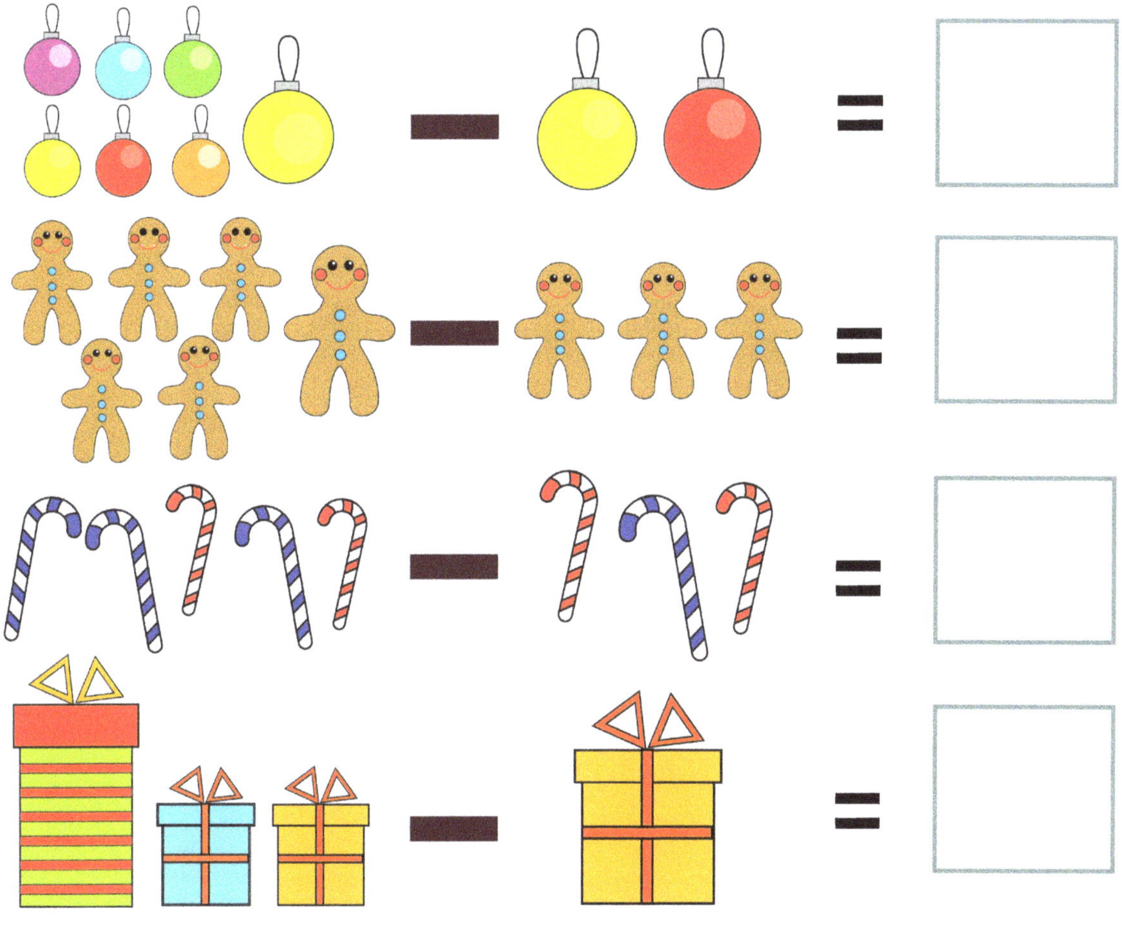

Activity No. 8

Find the Difference.

Activity No. 9

Find the Difference.

(10 triangles) − (3 triangles) = ☐

(8 circles) − (6 circles) = ☐

(6 hexagons) − (2 hexagons) = ☐

(8 diamonds) − (6 diamonds) = ☐

Activity No. 10

Find the Difference.

Activity No. 11

Use each subtraction equation to cross out the correct number of shapes to find the answer.

__7__ - __1__ = ____

2) 

__3__ - __0__ = ____

__9__ - __5__ = ____

4)

__10__ - __9__ = ____

Activity No. 12

Use each subtraction equation to cross out the correct number of shapes to find the answer.

9 - 9 = _____

6)

6 - 2 = _____

8 - 1 = _____

8)

3 - 3 = _____

Activity No. 13

Use each subtraction equation to cross out the correct number of shapes to find the answer.

8 - 2 = _____

△△△△

4 - 2 = _____

6 - 4 = _____

4) ⬛⬛⬛⬛⬛⬛

6 - 5 = _____

Activity No. 14

Use each subtraction equation to cross out the correct number of shapes to find the answer.

△△△△△△△△△

___9___ - ___3___ = ______

6) 

___4___ - ___3___ = ______

⬤⬤⬤⬤⬤⬤⬤

___7___ - ___5___ = ______

8) ⬤⬤⬤⬤⬤⬤⬤⬤⬤

___9___ - ___1___ = ______

Activity No. 15

Use each subtraction equation to cross out the correct number of shapes to find the answer.

___6___ - ___5___ = ______

10) ⬤ ⬤ ⬤ ⬤

___4___ - ___4___ = ______

___5___ - ___5___ = ______

4) ♡ ♡ ♡ ♡ ♡ ♡

___6___ - ___0___ = ______

Activity No. 16

Use each subtraction equation to cross out the correct number of shapes to find the answer.

__3__ - __1__ = ____

6) __7__ - __2__ = ____

__8__ - __0__ = ____

8) __8__ - __3__ = ____

Activity No. 17

Use each subtraction equation to cross out the correct number of shapes to find the answer.

_1_ - _1_ = _____

2) △△△△△△

_6_ - _5_ = _____

_9_ - _6_ = _____

6) ◇◇◇◇◇◇◇◇

_8_ - _1_ = _____

Activity No. 18

Use each subtraction equation to cross out the correct number of shapes to find the answer.

___4___ - ___1___ = _______

6) 

___8___ - ___1___ = _______

___7___ - ___3___ = _______

8)

___9___ - ___5___ = _______

Activity No. 19

Use each subtraction equation to cross out the correct number of shapes to find the answer.

___6___ - ___1___ = _______

2) 

___8___ - ___7___ = _______

___8___ - ___6___ = _______

4) ▲▲▲▲▲▲▲▲▲

___9___ - ___2___ = _______

Activity No. 20

Use each subtraction equation to cross out the correct number of shapes to find the answer.

8 - 2 = _____

8) ○○○

3 - 1 = _____

7 - 5 = _____

8) ◇◇◇◇◇◇

6 - 6 = _____

Activity No. 21

Find the Difference.

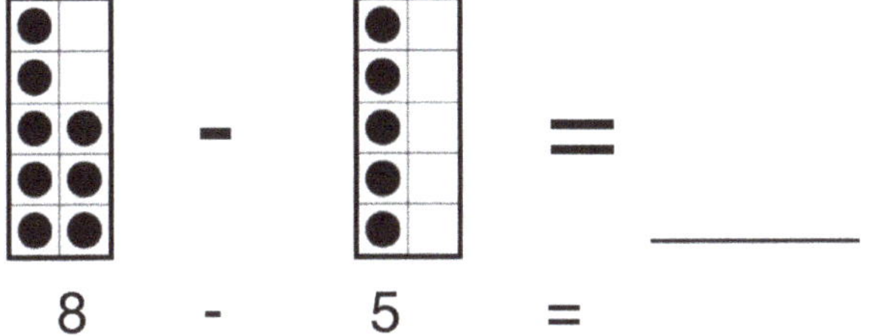

8 - 5 = _____

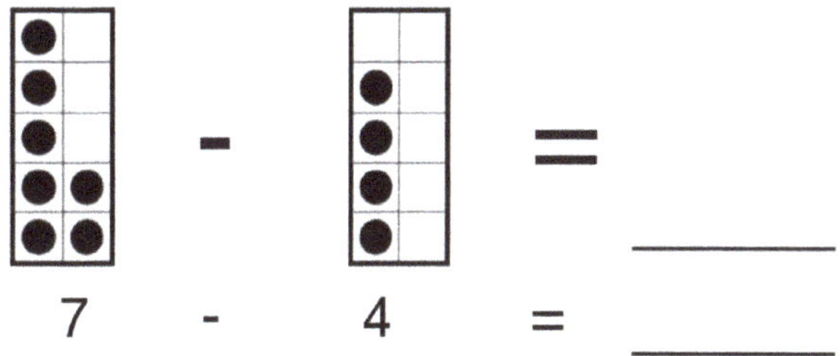

7 - 4 = _____

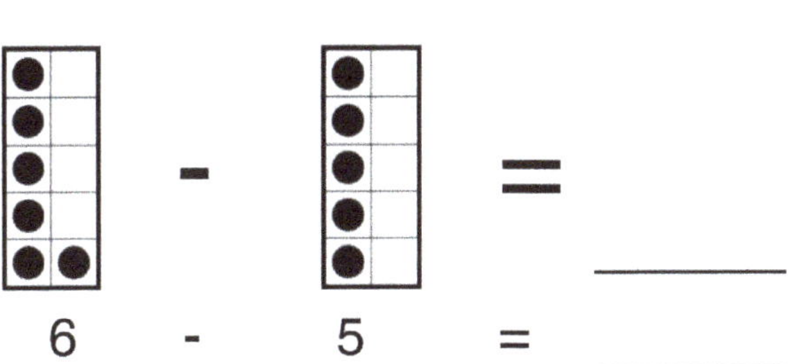

6 - 5 = _____

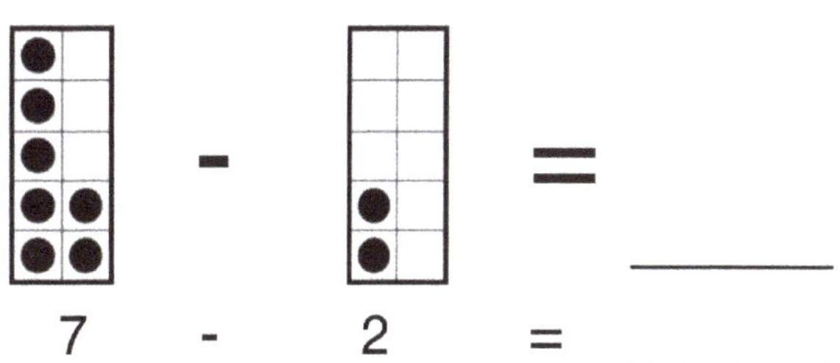

7 - 2 = _____

Activity No. 22

Find the Difference.

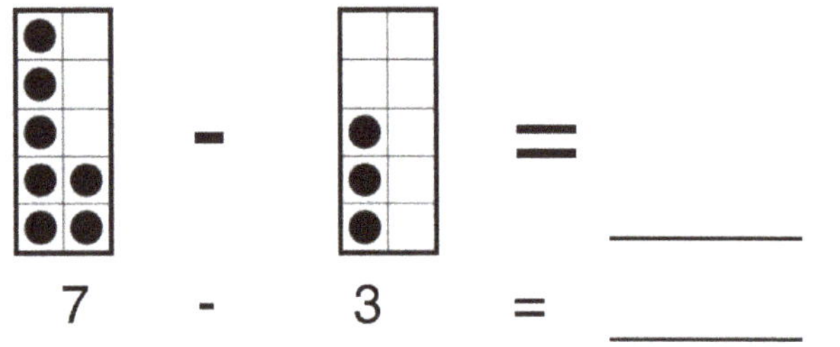

7   -   3   = _____

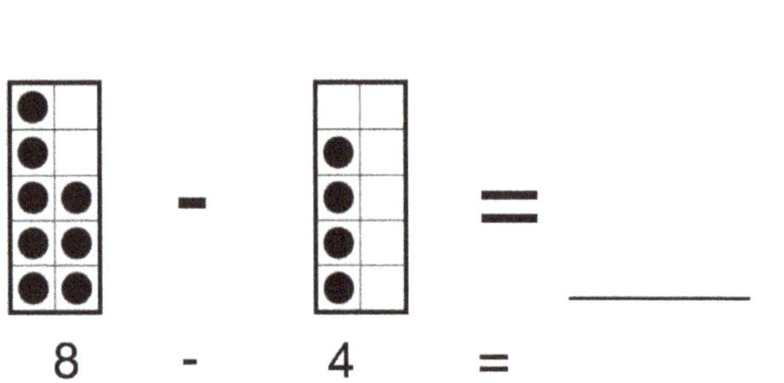

8   -   4   = _____

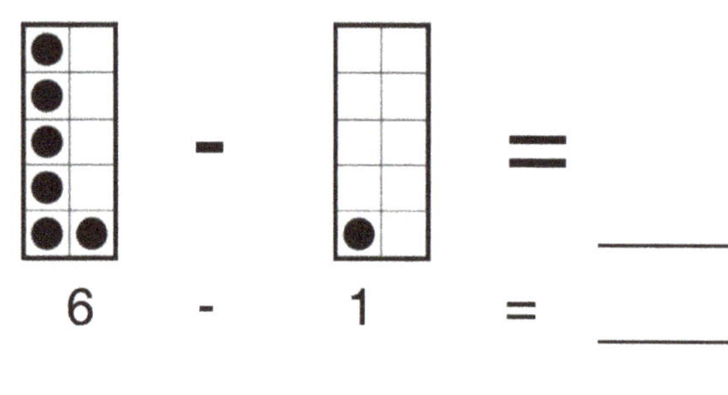

6   -   1   = _____

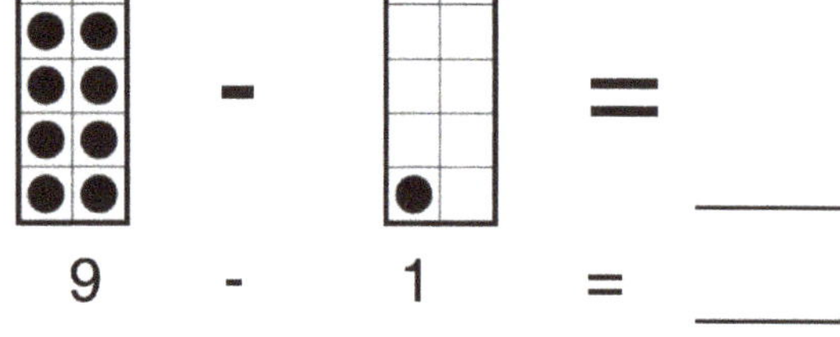

9   -   1   = _____

Activity No. 23

Find the Difference.

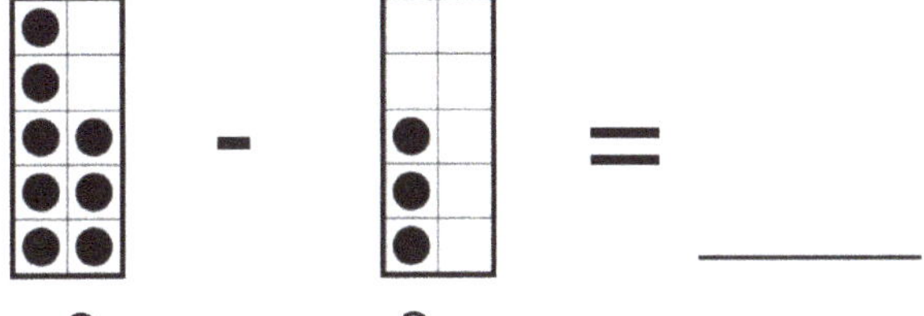

8 - 3 = _____

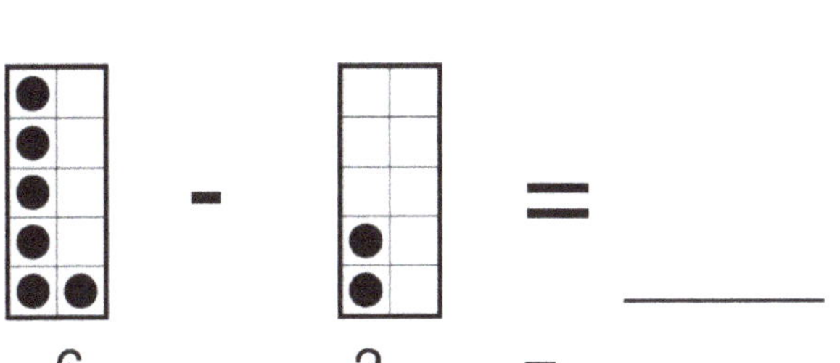

6 - 2 = _____

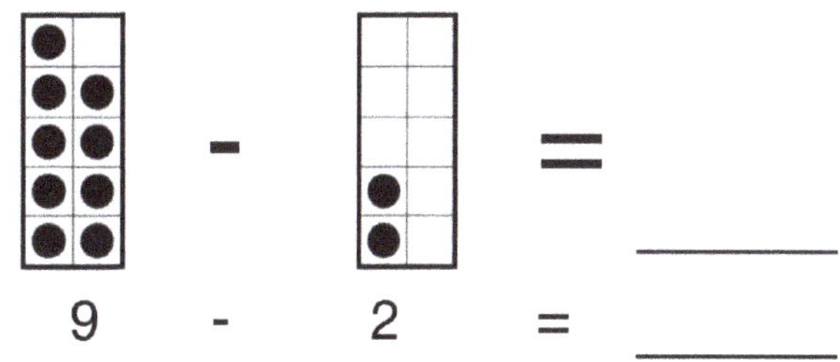

9 - 2 = _____

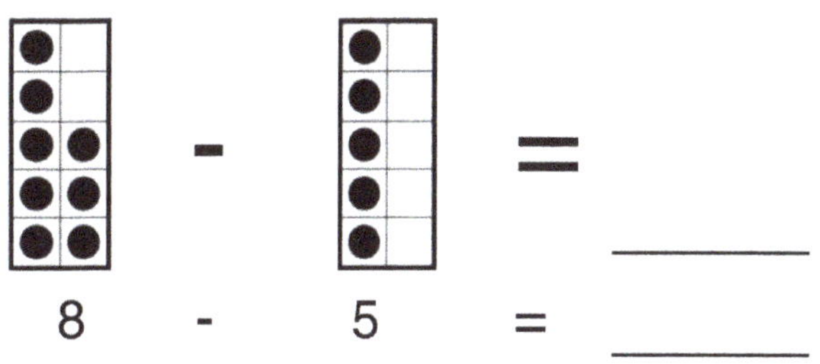

8 - 5 = _____

Activity No. 24

Find the Difference.

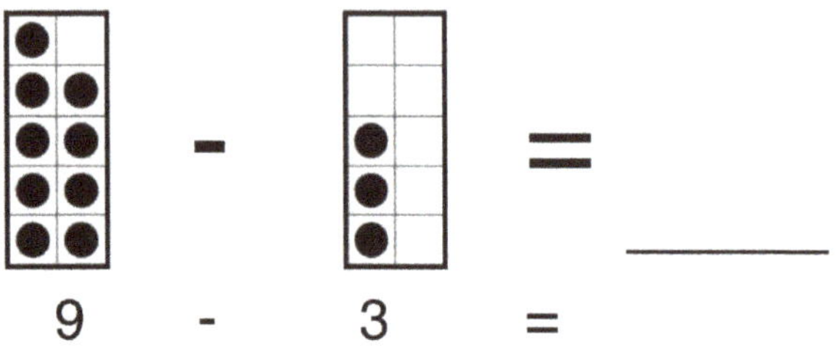

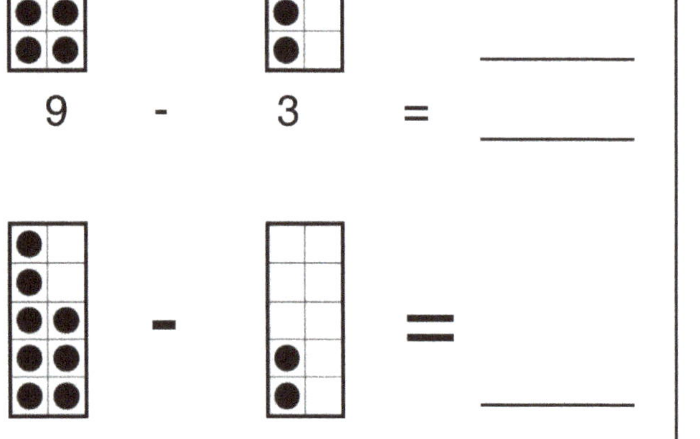

9   -   3   =   _____

8   -   2   =   _____

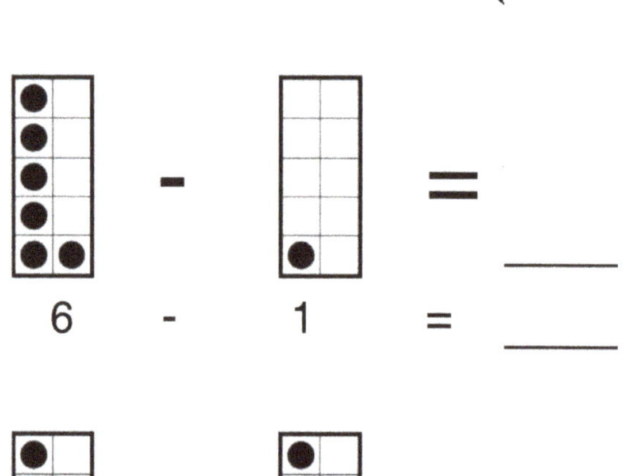

6   -   1   =   _____

9   -   5   =   _____

Activity No. 25

Find the Difference.

7 - 2	6 - 0	6 - 1
5 - 3	4 - 3	4 - 2

Activity No. 26

Find the Difference.

$$7 - 2$$

$$4 - 1$$

$$5 - 0$$

$$5 - 1$$

$$6 - 3$$

$$7 - 0$$

Activity No. 27

Find the Difference.

$$8 - 5 =$$

$$8 - 4 =$$

$$9 - 0 =$$

$$7 - 3 =$$

$$9 - 0 =$$

$$9 - 2 =$$

Activity No. 28

Find the Difference.

$$8 - 1 = \underline{}$$

$$7 - 4 = \underline{}$$

$$9 - 5 = \underline{}$$

$$7 - 2 = \underline{}$$

$$8 - 1 = \underline{}$$

$$7 - 3 = \underline{}$$

Activity No. 29

Find the Difference.

$$6 - 3$$

$$9 - 2$$

$$8 - 3$$

$$9 - 4$$

$$5 - 2$$

$$9 - 6$$

Activity No. 30

Find the Difference.

6	8	8
- 2	- 3	- 4

7	6	7
- 4	- 1	- 6

SINGLE DIGIT NUMBER SUBTRACTION EXERCISES

Activity No. 1

Find the Difference.

4 − 1 =

7 − 3 =

8 − 5 =

5 − 2 =

Find the Difference.

Activity No. 3

Find the Difference.

8 − 4 =

7 − 2 =

5 − 1 =

9 − 7 =

Activity No. 4

Find the Difference.

8 − 2 =

7 − 4 =

9 − 5 =

4 − 1 =

Activity No. 5

Find the Difference.

7 − 4 =

8 − 3 =

5 − 2 =

9 − 7 =

Activity No. 6

Find the Difference.

3 - 2	5 - 1	4 - 0
3 - 3	6 - 1	5 - 1

Activity No. 7

Find the Difference.

$$7 - 2 =$$

$$4 - 1 =$$

$$5 - 0 =$$

$$5 - 1 =$$

$$6 - 3 =$$

$$7 - 0 =$$

Find the Difference.

$$\begin{array}{r} 8 \\ -\ 1 \\ \hline \end{array} \qquad \begin{array}{r} 6 \\ -\ 1 \\ \hline \end{array} \qquad \begin{array}{r} 6 \\ -\ 2 \\ \hline \end{array}$$

$$\begin{array}{r} 5 \\ -\ 4 \\ \hline \end{array} \qquad \begin{array}{r} 7 \\ -\ 0 \\ \hline \end{array} \qquad \begin{array}{r} 5 \\ -\ 5 \\ \hline \end{array}$$

Activity No. 9

Find the Difference.

7	6	5
- 3	- 3	- 2

7	8	8
- 5	- 4	- 0

Find the Difference.

```
   4          6          5
 - 2        - 4        - 1
 ____       ____       ____


   6          8          6
 - 1        - 0        - 2
 ____       ____       ____
```

ANSWERS

Answers

VISUAL SUBTRACTION EXERCISES

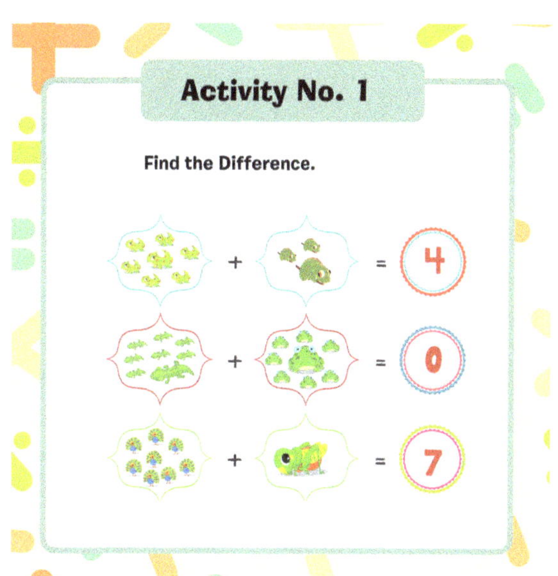

Answers

Activity No. 4
Find the Difference.
4
2
2

Activity No. 5
Find the Difference.
1
2
4
2

Activity No. 6
Find the Difference.
1
3
3
2

Activity No. 7
Find the Difference.
5
3
2
2

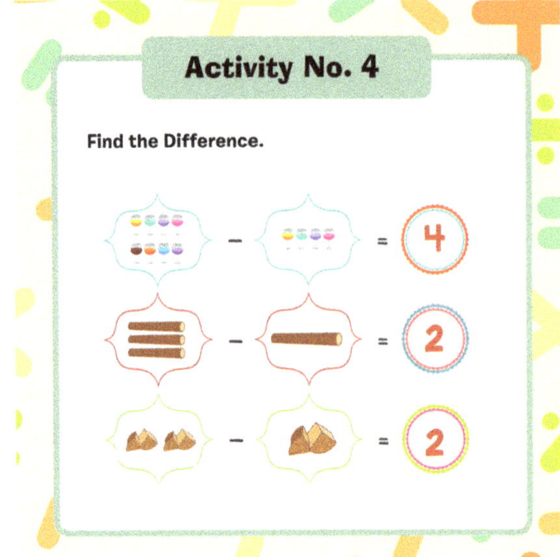

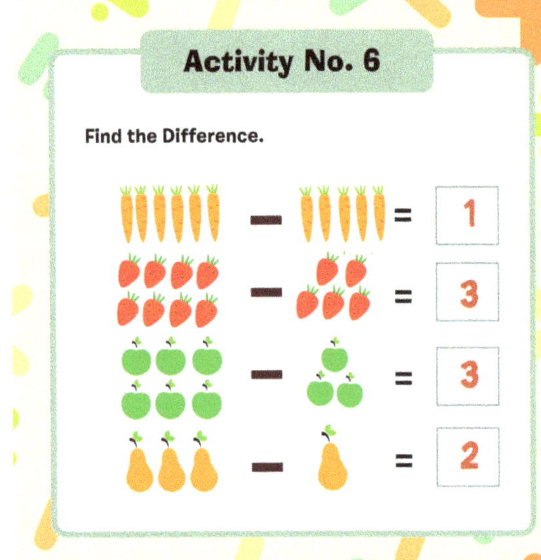

Answers

Activity No. 8

Find the Difference.

$$\blacksquare\ \blacksquare\ -\ \blacksquare\ =\ 1$$

$$-\ =\ 0$$

$$-\ =\ 4$$

$$-\ =\ 4$$

Activity No. 9

Find the Difference.

$$-\ =\ 6$$

$$-\ =\ 3$$

$$-\ =\ 4$$

$$-\ =\ 1$$

Activity No. 10

Find the Difference.

$$-\ =\ 2$$

$$-\ =\ 2$$

$$-\ =\ 2$$

$$-\ =\ 2$$

Activity No. 11

Use each subtraction equation to cross out the correct number of shapes to find the answer.

$$7 - 1 = 6$$

$$3 - 0 = 3$$

$$9 - 5 = 4$$

$$10 - 9 = 1$$

Answers

Activity No. 12

Use each subtraction equation to cross out the correct number of shapes to find the answer.

9 - 9 = 0

6 - 2 = 4

8 - 1 = 7

3 - 3 = 0

Activity No. 13

Use each subtraction equation to cross out the correct number of shapes to find the answer.

8 - 2 = 6

4 - 2 = 2

6 - 4 = 2

6 - 5 = 1

Activity No. 14

Use each subtraction equation to cross out the correct number of shapes to find the answer.

9 - 3 = 6

4 - 3 = 1

7 - 5 = 2

9 - 1 = 8

Activity No. 15

Use each subtraction equation to cross out the correct number of shapes to find the answer.

6 - 5 = 1

4 - 4 = 0

5 - 5 = 0

6 - 0 = 6

Answers

Activity No. 16

Use each subtraction equation to cross out the correct number of shapes to find the answer.

3 - 1 = 2

7 - 2 = 5

8 - 0 = 8

8 - 3 = 5

Activity No. 17

Use each subtraction equation to cross out the correct number of shapes to find the answer.

1 - 1 = 0

6 - 5 = 1

9 - 6 = 3

8 - 1 = 7

Activity No. 18

Use each subtraction equation to cross out the correct number of shapes to find the answer.

4 - 1 = 3

8 - 1 = 7

7 - 3 = 4

9 - 5 = 4

Activity No. 19

Use each subtraction equation to cross out the correct number of shapes to find the answer.

6 - 1 = 5

8 - 7 = 1

8 - 6 = 2

9 - 2 = 7

Answers

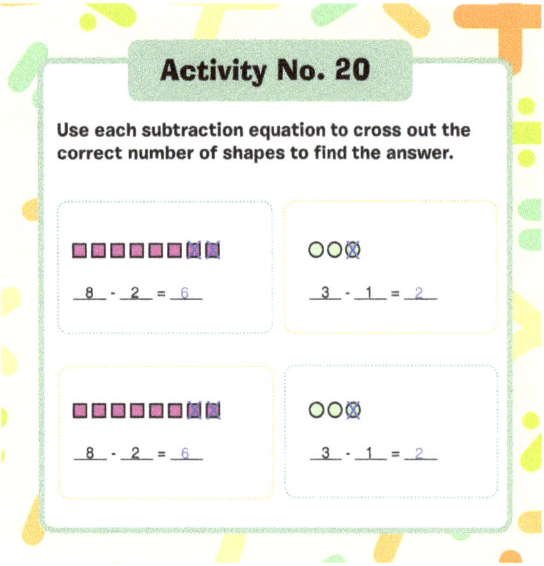

Activity No. 20

Use each subtraction equation to cross out the correct number of shapes to find the answer.

8 - 2 = 6

3 - 1 = 2

8 - 2 = 6

3 - 1 = 2

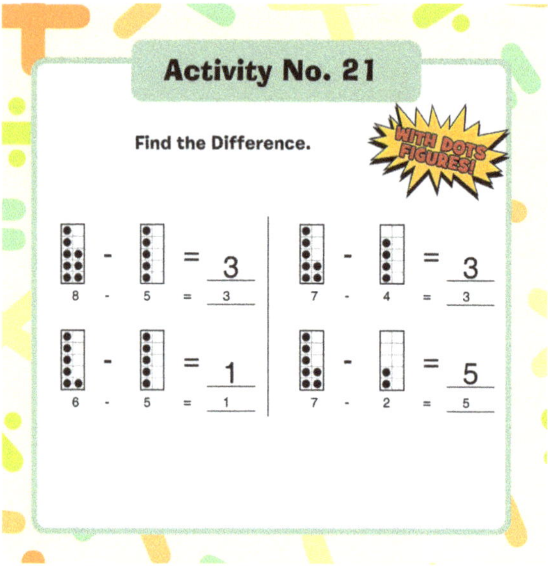

Activity No. 21

Find the Difference.

WITH DOTS FIGURES!

8 - 5 = 3

7 - 4 = 3

6 - 5 = 1

7 - 2 = 5

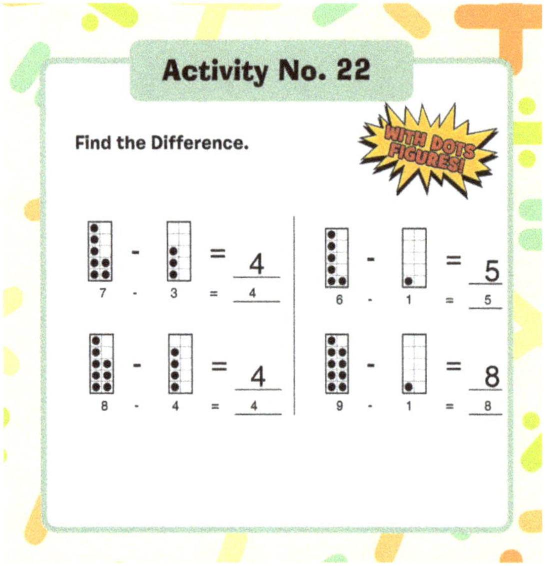

Activity No. 22

Find the Difference.

WITH DOTS FIGURES!

7 - 3 = 4

6 - 1 = 5

8 - 4 = 4

9 - 1 = 8

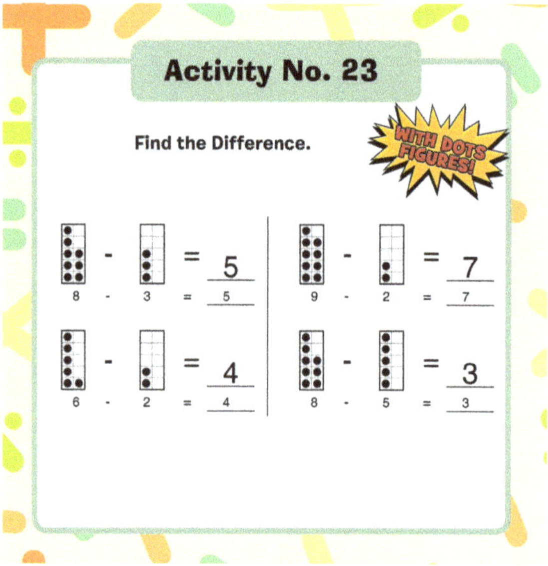

Activity No. 23

Find the Difference.

WITH DOTS FIGURES!

8 - 3 = 5

9 - 2 = 7

6 - 2 = 4

8 - 5 = 3

Answers

Activity No. 24

Find the Difference.

9 − 3 = 6

6 − 1 = 5

8 − 2 = 6

9 − 5 = 4

Activity No. 25

Find the Difference.

$$\begin{array}{r} 7 \\ -\ 2 \\ \hline 5 \end{array} \qquad \begin{array}{r} 6 \\ -\ 0 \\ \hline 6 \end{array} \qquad \begin{array}{r} 6 \\ -\ 1 \\ \hline 5 \end{array}$$

$$\begin{array}{r} 5 \\ -\ 3 \\ \hline 2 \end{array} \qquad \begin{array}{r} 4 \\ -\ 3 \\ \hline 1 \end{array} \qquad \begin{array}{r} 4 \\ -\ 2 \\ \hline 2 \end{array}$$

Activity No. 26

Find the Difference.

$$\begin{array}{r} 7 \\ -\ 2 \\ \hline 5 \end{array} \qquad \begin{array}{r} 4 \\ -\ 1 \\ \hline 3 \end{array} \qquad \begin{array}{r} 5 \\ -\ 0 \\ \hline 5 \end{array}$$

$$\begin{array}{r} 5 \\ -\ 1 \\ \hline 4 \end{array} \qquad \begin{array}{r} 6 \\ -\ 3 \\ \hline 3 \end{array} \qquad \begin{array}{r} 7 \\ -\ 0 \\ \hline 7 \end{array}$$

Activity No. 27

Find the Difference.

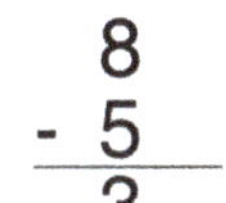

$$\begin{array}{r} 8 \\ -\ 5 \\ \hline 3 \end{array} \qquad \begin{array}{r} 8 \\ -\ 4 \\ \hline 4 \end{array} \qquad \begin{array}{r} 9 \\ -\ 0 \\ \hline 9 \end{array}$$

$$\begin{array}{r} 7 \\ -\ 3 \\ \hline 4 \end{array} \qquad \begin{array}{r} 9 \\ -\ 0 \\ \hline 9 \end{array} \qquad \begin{array}{r} 9 \\ -\ 2 \\ \hline 7 \end{array}$$

Answers

Activity No. 28

Find the Difference.

8 − 1 **7**	7 − 4 **3**	9 − 5 **4**
7 − 2 **5**	8 − 1 **7**	7 − 3 **4**

Activity No. 29

Find the Difference.

6 − 3 **3**	9 − 2 **7**	8 − 3 **5**
9 − 4 **5**	5 − 2 **3**	9 − 6 **3**

Activity No. 30

Find the Difference.

6 − 2 **4**	8 − 3 **5**	8 − 4 **4**
7 − 4 **3**	6 − 1 **5**	7 − 6 **1**

Answers

Activity No. 1

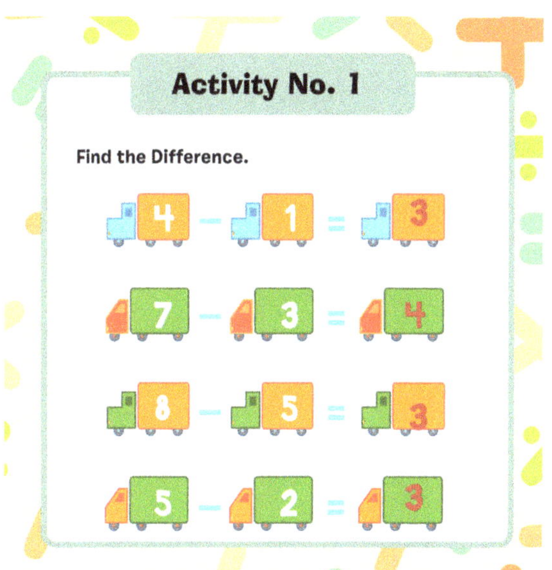

Find the Difference.

4 − 1 = 3

7 − 3 = 4

8 − 5 = 3

5 − 2 = 3

Activity No. 2

Find the Difference.

8 − 7 = 1

4 − 2 = 2

9 − 3 = 6

6 − 1 = 5

Activity No. 3

Find the Difference.

8 − 4 = 4

7 − 2 = 5

5 − 1 = 4

9 − 7 = 2

Answers

Activity No. 4

Find the Difference.

$8 - 2 = 6$

$7 - 4 = 3$

$9 - 5 = 4$

$4 - 1 = 3$

Activity No. 6

Find the Difference.

$$\begin{array}{r} 3 \\ -\ 2 \\ \hline 1 \end{array} \qquad \begin{array}{r} 5 \\ -\ 1 \\ \hline 4 \end{array} \qquad \begin{array}{r} 4 \\ -\ 0 \\ \hline 4 \end{array}$$

$$\begin{array}{r} 3 \\ -\ 3 \\ \hline 0 \end{array} \qquad \begin{array}{r} 6 \\ -\ 1 \\ \hline 5 \end{array} \qquad \begin{array}{r} 5 \\ -\ 1 \\ \hline 4 \end{array}$$

Activity No. 5

Find the Difference.

$7 - 4 = 3$

$8 - 3 = 5$

$5 - 2 = 3$

$9 - 7 = 2$

Activity No. 7

Find the Difference.

$$\begin{array}{r} 7 \\ -\ 2 \\ \hline 5 \end{array} \qquad \begin{array}{r} 4 \\ -\ 1 \\ \hline 3 \end{array} \qquad \begin{array}{r} 5 \\ -\ 0 \\ \hline 5 \end{array}$$

$$\begin{array}{r} 5 \\ -\ 1 \\ \hline 4 \end{array} \qquad \begin{array}{r} 6 \\ -\ 3 \\ \hline 3 \end{array} \qquad \begin{array}{r} 7 \\ -\ 0 \\ \hline 7 \end{array}$$

Activity No. 8

Find the Difference.

8 − 1 = 7	6 − 1 = 5	6 − 2 = 4
5 − 4 = 1	7 − 0 = 7	5 − 5 = 0

Activity No. 9

Find the Difference.

7 − 3 = 4	6 − 3 = 3	5 − 2 = 3
7 − 5 = 2	8 − 4 = 4	8 − 0 = 8

Activity No. 10

Find the Difference.

4 − 2 = 2	6 − 4 = 2	5 − 1 = 4
6 − 1 = 5	8 − 0 = 8	6 − 2 = 4

Visit
BABY PROFESSOR
EDUCATION KIDS
www.BabyProfessorBooks.com
to download Free Baby Professor eBooks and view
our catalog of new and exciting Children's Books